Apocalypse of Youth

Apocalypse of Youth

The memoirs of
Harriet Lorence Nesbitt
as told to Olga Soler

Edited by Jeanne C. DeFazio

Foreword by Julia C. Davis

RESOURCE *Publications* • Eugene, Oregon

APOCALYPSE OF YOUTH

Resource Publications
An Imprint of Wipf and Stock Publishers
199 W. 8th Ave., Suite 3
Eugene, OR 97401

www.wipfandstock.com

PAPERBACK ISBN: 979-8-3852-6607-4
HARDCOVER ISBN: 979-8-3852-6608-1
EBOOK ISBN: 979-8-3852-6609-8

VERSION NUMBER 010226

This book is dedicated to my sons, New York City attorney Roger Lorence and the belated Larry Nesbitt. Both bright lights who have made this world a better place.

—Harriet Lorence Nesbitt

Julia C. Davis

Empowering English Language Learners, contributing author

Specialist Fourth Class John Joseph DeFazio: Advocating For Disabled American Veterans, contributing author

An Artistic Tribute to Harriet Tubman, co-editor

The Commission, contributing author

Finding A Better Way, contributing author

The Christian World Liberation Front, contributing author

Jesus Among the Homeless, contributing author

Otto & The White Dove, contributing author

Letting Go, contributing author

The Journey Home, contributing author

Media Fellowship International, contributing author

Jeanne C. DeFazio

Creative Ways to Build Christian Community, ed. with John P. Lathrop

How to Have an Attitude of Gratitude on the Night Shift, co-author with Teresa Flowers

Redeeming the Screens, ed. with William David Spencer

Berkeley Street Theatre: How Improvisation and Street Theater Emerged as Christian Outreach to the Culture of the Time, editor

Empowering English Language Learners, ed. with William David Spencer

Keeping the Dream Alive: A Reflection on the Art of Harriet Lorence Nesbitt, author and editor

Specialist Fourth Class John Joseph DeFazio: Advocating for Disabled American Veterans, editor

Christian Egalitarian Leadership, contributing author

An Artistic Tribute to Harriet Tubman, co-editor

The Commission, editor

Finding a Better Way, editor

The Christian World Liberation Front, author

Jesus Among the Homeless, contributing author

Otto & The White Dove, editor

Letting Go, co-author with Terry McDermott

The Journey Home, author

Media Fellowship International, co-editor with Susan G. Stafford

Olga Soler

Just Don't Marry One: Interracial Dating, Marriage, and Parenting, contributing author

Tough Inspirations from the Weeping Prophet, author

Apocalypse of Youth, author

Creative Ways to Build Christian Community, contributing author

Epistle to the Magdalenes, author and illustrator

Redeeming the Screens: Living Stories of Media "Ministers" Bringing the Message of Jesus Christ to the Entertainment Industry, contributing author

Berkeley Street Theatre: How Improvisation and Street Theater Emerged as Christian Outreach to the Culture of the Time, contributing author

The first book: *Nature*; the second book: *Scripture*; the third book: *Christ Time Travel Series*, author

First book: *Frankie*, second book: *Frankie: Pestilence, Frankie: Holocaust, The Frankenstein Series*, author

Primer for Home Fellowship, author

Empowering English Language Learners: Successful Strategies of Christian Educators, contributing author

Keeping the Dream Alive: A Reflection on the Art of Harriet Lorence Nesbitt, contributing author

An Artistic Tribute to Harriet Tubman, contributing artist

The Commission: The God Who Calls Us to Be a Voice during a Pandemic, Wildfires, and Racial Violence, contributing author

Finding a Better Way, contributing author

Jesus Among the Homeless, contributing author

The Journey Home, contributing author

Contents

Acknowledgments

A LOT OF HARD work went into making this book. It was inspired by the creative genius of all the talents fondly mentioned in these pages. I would like to acknowledge my nephew Michael Nesbitt and his wife Martha who have been very supportive of me. I owe a debt of gratitude to all those who nagged me over the years to tell my story. Jeanne DeFazio has been a wonderful friend. I am grateful to Mary Riso and to Richard Bruce who helped me edit this work and to Olga Soler for taking on this project. Special thanks to Caleb Loring III, Peter Lynch, Governor Jerry Brown and Senator Rockefeller for their support of this work.

Foreword

Julia C. Davis

I HAD THE HONOR to contribute a foreword to *Keeping The Dream Alive: Reflections On The Art Of Harriet Lorence Nesbitt.* I was asked to write a brief foreword in the reprinting of this book. I looked at the painting *Apocalypse of Youth* and read Harriet Nesbitt's description of it in her introduction: "*Apocalypse of Youth* is my artistic comment on the pitfalls of youth in a millennial society."[1] When I read Harriet's words, the tragedy of the August 27, 2025 shooting at Annunciation Catholic Church in Minneapolis, Minnesota flashed into my mind."[2]

As an African American teacher with years of experience teaching mainstream, special education and "at risk" students, I know first hand how easily violence erupts in the inner city classroom and innocent victims become statistics. We must break this cycle of anger and manic violence in and out of the classroom. Our nation is grieving over the senseless repeated slaughter of the innocent. I prayed for the victims and their families, recalling

1. Nesbitt, Soler, *Apocalypse of Youth*, xvii.
2. Forrester, Meg. "What We Know About The Minnesota School Shooting Suspect Robin Westman," August 28, 2025, ABC News.

the promise of Psalm 34:18: "The Lord is close to the brokenhearted and saves those who are crushed in spirit." I prayed for God to give our national and community leaders, educators and local protective services wisdom and strategies for justice and change relying on the words of the prophet Amos chapter 5, verse 4: "But let justice roll on like a river, righteousness like a never-failing stream!" I pray in Jesus Name for an end to the violence against innocent children gathered in prayer: Lord don't let these children die in vain. Let their memories spark change in our nation. Harriet Nesbitt lost her gifted son Larry who struggled with a psychological disorder. He was released from a halfway house and run down on a highway road. As founder of Mother's For More Halfway Houses, Harriet fiercely advocated for the needs of the mentally ill so the death of her own son and others like him would not die in vain. God bless you Harriet for modeling faith active in love according to James 2:18: "Show me your faith without deeds, and I will show you my faith by my deeds."

Preface

IT IS THE MISSION of "Leap Over the Edge" Productions to bring to light what can be accomplished by ordinary individuals through faith and through whatever creative means they find in their path. Obstacles, problems, issues, gifts and inheritance of a good or bad nature can all be used to fight the ills of our world if the attitude of the artist is right. Harriet Nesbitt has that right kind of an attitude.

She, like the rest of us, is more than the sum of her parts but the part she shared with the world in her art as well as in her publication of *Politics and Such* has quietly influenced many movers and shakers to awareness and action. Now retired she continues to open our eyes, in language we can all understand, to issues that affect us all.

As Picasso exemplified all the horrors of war in one mural he christened *Guernica* so she in her *Apocalypse* illustrates succinctly the thousands of conflicts of one who has survived the maelstrom of social change in the last 80 years. The perils humanity has survived during this time have very nearly produced an apocalypse many times, not only of youth but of hope. Yet hope is resilient as Harriet shows us through people of worth like those she has had the pleasure of interviewing.

Personally having experienced some of the things that have caused her great agitation through the civil rights milestones of the 70s, the trials of urban poverty and the concerns of environmental, technological and political upheaval, I am warmed by the quiet but powerful way she has gathered her influence and put it where it can do the most good with a most intriguing set of people. We hope you will be as moved by this book as we were when we read it.

May Harriet give us many more years of her feisty, inspiring and poignant point of view.

Olga Soler—Director
"Leap Over the Edge Productions"

Apocalypse of Youth

Introduction

APOCALYPSE OF YOUTH IS my artistic comment on the pitfalls of youth in a millennial society. It is a collage of imagery which include a Rolls Royce, the closing of New York City's 68th Street baby orphanage, John the Divine's four horsemen of the apocalypse from the Book of Revelation, a scene from the epic disaster *Three Mile Island*, planes dropping bombs, Jesus and Mary blessing youth, a student with a blue Three Mile Island sweater riding a red demonic horse next to a boy on a horse.

The boy on the horse was painted in the likeness of my beloved son Larry. Larry attended Franklin Marshall College within the vicinity of the Three Mile Island's volcano eruption. Larry and I talked about everything. When the ideas poured out in our conversations, he repeated this mantra over and over again: *Paint, mom, paint*! I can hear his words in my heart.

Mothers for More Halfway Houses

I founded the non-profit Mothers for More Half Way Houses[3] after the tragic death of my gifted teenage son Larry. Larry was a savant in mathematics with a 100% average with or without a computer. At graduation from prep school, Larry received first prize from Ted Kennedy in writing and mathematics. He attended Franklin Marshall College receiving high honors. Sadly, Larry's life was cut short in a tragic accident. He suffered from bipolar depression and was released from a halfway house in an unstable condition and was run down in the road by an oncoming car. Larry's death was devastating but because of it, I founded Mothers for More Halfway Houses to advocate for availability of housing for those suffering from mental illness. My passion and commitment to bring focus to the cause continues. I never want any child suffering from mental illness to die unnecessarily for lack of supervised care and housing.

Jeanne DeFazio has been one of MMHH's sparkplugs. A true friend, Jeanne has supported MMHH since its inception. She understood that personal heartache was the impetus of MMHH, persuaded our mutual friend Michael P. Grace II to support MMHH, and served as a patron for several MMHH events. Jeanne also assisted me with the column *Politics and Such* from 1996–1998 attending New York events getting photos and comments from distinguished celebrities. She enjoyed meeting philanthropists who had a passion and energy for making a difference.

3. http://www.charityblossom.org/nonprofit/mothers-for-more-halfway-houses-inc-new-york-ny-10065-harriet-nesbitt-133229931/.

Jeanne and I reviewed editions of *Politics and Such* organizing this work to reflect on critical social issues of the past two decades:

In 1986, Dorothy Frooks featured a front page article in the *Murray Hill News* entitled "Her Dream Needs Realism." Dorothy's article endorsed Mothers For More Halfway Houses and described me as an artist, social activist and aristocrat who had a dream.[4] I have identified that dream in this book hoping that readers will embrace it to find greater happiness and purpose in life.

I was the author of the column, *Politics and Such* published by the *Murray Hill News* owned by the Dorothy Frooks[5] and her husband, Jay Vanderbilt. I interviewed celebrities at New York City events reflecting on matters of social significance. I met Mrs. Frooks (who holds the distinction of being the first woman admitted to the New York State Bar) through my late father Judge Louis Lorence. As Mrs. Frooks described, I am a New York artist who has lived a well publicized life mingling with distinguished members of New York society.

In February 1958, *The Palm Beach Daily News* caption read: *Harriet Lorence, daughter of Judge Louis Lorence of New York, is currently working on a painting of the West Palm Beach Polo Club...In New York she has a studio at 49 West 57th Street.* A well educated and known artist, I am the daughter of Judge Louis Lorence. The *New York Times* listed my father as a graduate of New York University Law School with a Masters in Law. He was the first judge to be featured on a television program. Louis Lorence initiated and enforced the New York State and Floridian

4. *Her Dream Needs Realism*, Dorothy Frooks, Murray Hill News. 1986.

5. Dorothy Frooks (February 12, 1896 – April 13, 1997) published the *Murray Hill News* in 1952.

Extradition Law. In an online feature entitled *Seduction of the Innocent*, the author, E.H. Chapin, reflects on inner city gang related violence due to the influence of popular comic books published with advertisements of the sale of guns and knives. Chapin details Domestic Relations Justice Louis Lorence suggestion for Federal legislation to bar interstate advertisements and sale of knives and toy weapons that can be converted and used as real weapons:

> *Seduction of the Innocent: The Devil's Allies The Struggle Against the Comic Book Industry Neutral men are the devil's allies.- E.H. Chapin:*
>
> *The Federal Government has laws restricting interstate commerce under certain circumstances injurious to the people. Could not such laws be made to include the shipment of objectionable comic books? Assistant District Attorney John E. Cone, who has investigated teen-age gangs, has stated as a result of his findings that crime comic books should be "done away with because not only do they list advertisements through which guns can easily be purchased by juveniles, but they give a synthetic thrill which kids cannot fulfill in real life without actually committing crime." The suggestion for Federal legislation to bar interstate advertisements and sale of knives and toy weapons that can be converted was made by Domestic Relations Justice Louis Lorence. Hundreds and hundreds of such illegal weapons have been confiscated by the police in New York. "For a number of years," Judge Lorence stated, "all over the city boys have approached other students in schools and have demanded money for protection. If money is not given, beatings often ensue. In the past two months, particularly, there were many cases in my court where parents complained of this protection racket." I myself*

> *have seen more than twenty-five children who*
> *have either been victims of such threats or have*
> *played the racket game themselves, usually with*
> *switch blade knives. Although switchblade knives*
> *serve no purpose except quick violence, they are*
> *still advertised in comic books for the youngest*
> *children.*[6]

Like my father, I have a strong sense of social ethics and justice and I understand the power of the printed word. My editions of *Politics and Such* reflect regard for the ruling class but resonate with concern for the down and out and most vulnerable in society:

Chapter One: *Without passion you don't have energy; without energy you have nothing.* Donald Trump's quote provides the perfect opportunity to reflect on the issues that challenged our globe twenty years ago and still present a challenge in the millennial era.

Chapter Two: *We will be judged as a society by how we treat the most vulnerable* expresses my deep concern for the marginalized and needy throughout the nation and the world.

Chapter Three: *Social Media is the predictor of the Postmodern Age* explains the benefits and the dangers of the postmodern era where elections are fought, won or lost by the power of the written word on Twitter.

Chapter Four: *Politics and Such 1996 list of the most fascinating women* extols the advancement of women in the past twenty years reflecting on the lives of remarkable women who left a legacy of accomplishment.

Conclusion: *In spite of it all, I still believe that it is the best of all possible worlds.* A personal tragedy gave me the

6. E H. Chapin, *Seduction of the Innocent*, www.dreadfuldays. net/soti/soti_chapt12/soti_chapt12.html.

opportunity to realize a dream and make a difference in the lives of others.

Many of the individuals interviewed and photographed for *Politics and Such* have died. This book is a tribute to those who have gone on but left a legacy that made a difference. I am happy to be able to present stories of these celebrities and philanthropists who have contributed so much! I know that they will be an encouragement to you as you meet them in this book, or deepen your relationship with them if you have already enjoyed their work.

Harriet Nesbitt

The young Harriet Nesbitt on a ladder
in front of Symphony Americana[1]

1. "The young Harriet Lorence Nesbitt on a ladder in front of *Symphony Americana.*"

"She [Harriet Nesbitt] painted *Symphony Americana* because she believed that Van Cliburn's Russian concerts eased tensions between the Soviet Union and the United States during the Cold War. *Symphony Americana* demonstrates the creative power of art to unite humankind." DeFazio, *Keeping The Dream Alive*, 5.

CHAPTER ONE

Without passion you don't have energy;
without energy you have nothing.[1]

Donald Trump

IN 2016, DONALD TRUMP made history by winning the Republican Party's nomination for President of the United States. His political approach is controversial but he and his opponent, Hillary Clinton, have succeeded in injecting energy and passion into the 2016 election. Regardless of the outcome in the 2016 general election, Trump is a charismatic leader who will leave a legacy as an entertainer, billionaire class businessman and philanthropist. I met and interviewed Mr. Trump several times for *Politics and Such*. I recall his graciousness as he invited me, photographer Joanne La Placa and Jeanne DeFazio to cover events.

1. "Donald Trump," Brainy Quote, accessed September 19, 2016, http://www.brainyquote.com/quotes/authors/d/donald_trump_2.html#z3TtPvlsu5Umi2QS.99.

I interviewed Hillary Clinton in Saratoga. In the April 1996 edition of *Politics and Such*, I applauded *Hilary Clinton for taking on the AMA and caring that every American should have Health Care.*[2]

Mrs. Hilary Rodham Clinton is a controversial woman who has taken on foreign and domestic policy issues with great passion, energy and focus. *She served as the 67th United States Secretary of State in the administration of President Barack Obama, as a United States Senator for New York from 2001 to 2009 and as the wife of the 42nd President of the United States, Bill Clinton, as First Lady from 1993 to 2001.*[3]

As a woman, Hillary Clinton's public service is unrivaled in United States history. In 2016, she made history as the first woman nominated by a major party for the United States presidency.

Between 1996–1998, *Politics and Such* ran interviews and photos of Donald Trump and Secretary Hillary Clinton. It has been an honor for me to meet and write about both of these controversial and remarkable United States citizens. I tell all of my friends how grateful I am to be alive to see the outcome of this election.

Mother Teresa was at the top of the most fascinating women's list *Politics and Such* for 1996. *Politics and Such* annually acknowledged women who advanced the cause of womanhood from many perspectives. Each of the women mentioned displayed great passion and energy in their various efforts and made a difference.

In the early 1990s, at the dedication of her Bronx (New York) community, Michael P. Grace II introduced

2. Harriet Nesbitt, *Politics and Such*, "*The Murray Hill News*, April 1996.

3. Wikipedia, Hilary Clinton, https://en.wikipedia.org/wiki/Hillary_Clinton.

me to Mother Teresa. She blessed me and my work as founder of *Mothers For More Halfway Houses*. *St. Teresa of Calcutta, (1910–1997), was an Albanian–born Indian Roman Catholic nun who founded the Missionaries of Charity, a Roman Catholic religious congregation. Members of the Missionaries of Charity adhere to the vows of chastity, poverty and obedience, and the fourth vow, to give whole-hearted and free service to the poorest of the poor.*[4]

In *Politics and Such* (April 1996) I praised *Mother Teresa whose commitment to humanity is evidence of the androgyny of God.*[5] Mother Teresa's impact is undeniable. On September 4, 2016, she was canonized by the Roman Catholic Church. In her Nobel Prize acceptance speech, she declared:

> *. . . at the hour of death we are going to be judged on what we have been to the poor, to the hungry, naked, the homeless, and he (Jesus) makes himself that hungry one, that naked one, that homeless one, not only hungry for bread, but hungry for love, not only naked for a piece of cloth, but naked of that human dignity, not only homeless for a room to live, but homeless for that being forgotten, been unloved, uncared, being nobody to nobody, having forgotten what is human love,*

4. "St. Teresa of Calcutta, (1910–1997), was an Albanian–born Indian Roman Catholic nun who founded the Missionaries of Charity, a Roman Catholic religious congregation." Wikipedia, *The Free Encyclopedia*, s.v. "Mother Teresa," accessed September 19, 2016, https://en.m.wikepedia.org/wiki/Mother Teresa.

"Members of the Missionaries of Charity adhere to the vows of chastity, poverty and obedience, and the fourth vow, to give wholehearted and free service to the poorest of the poor." Wikipedia, Missionaries of Charity, https://en.wikipedia.org/wiki/Missionaries_of_Charity.

5. Harriet Nesbitt, *Politics and Such*, *The Murray Hill News*, April 1997.

> *what is human touch, what is to be loved by*
> *somebody, and he says: Whatever you did to the*
> *least of these my brethren, you did it to me.*[6]

In my prophetic artwork, *Doom and Gloom* (2008), President Obama points to two asteroids seen over Norway. The doom and gloom of Star Wars' predictions pale by comparison in the face of the horror of racial inner city violence in the past 8 years. During President Obama's administration, racial discrimination and violence intensified in the inner cities of the United States. This concerns me deeply as a US citizen and social columnist. After attending the twenty-ninth annual Urban League Luncheon at the Plaza, I expressed the need for social and economic justice: (April 1998 edition of *Politics and Such*):

> *Martin Luther King was well represented by*
> *the 29th Urban League annual luncheon at the*
> *Plaza, with Mayor and Mrs. Dinkins, who flew*
> *in from their home in Rome, Italy. The event was*
> *chaired by former Congressman Bill Greene and*
> *the gracious Laquita Henry. The theme of the*
> *event was that when any member of our society*
> *suffers from social and economic justice the en-*
> *tire society suffers.*[7]

Every United States citizen is suffering because of racial injustice and violence in our inner cities. Domestic violence and terrorism are critical issues in the 2016 election. As a social columnist I focused on the need for racial

6. "Mother Teresa—Acceptance Speech," Nobelprize.org, accessed September 19, 2016, http://www.nobelprize.org/nobel_prizes/peace/laureates/1979/teresa-acceptance.html.*www*.

7. Harriet Nesbitt, *Politics and Such. The Murray Hill News*, April 1998.

equality. I made it a point to write about organizations that supported the advancement of African Americans.

I reported on the New York Urban League[8] and the distinguished members of this African American society who made a difference in the lives of those marginalized by racial barriers. *Politics and Such* covered the twenty-ninth NYC Urban League luncheon where the late Congressman Greene (then Ronald O. Perelman's government liaison at MacAndrews and Forbes), prominent African American activist LaQuita Henry and Mayor Dinkins passionately supported the Urban League's efforts to provide opportunity for all Americans.

Politics and Such covered the 1998 Congress of Racial Equality (CORE)[9] annual Ambassadorial Reception and Awards Dinner in New York City. In observance of the Martin Luther King Federal Holiday, the event brought over two thousand together in an effort to promote racial equality. CORE's twenty-ninth annual Martin Luther King Jr. Ambassadorial Reception and Awards Dinner took place ten years prior (January 1998) to the inauguration of President Barack Obama as the first United States President of African descent. The leaders presiding were devoted to racial equality. The April 1998 edition of *Politics and Such* extolled these giants who paved the way for the election of President Obama.

In 2015, footage of savage and brutal ISIS beheadings went viral on the internet and television. Millennial ISIS beheadings demonstrate a critical need for a global unified defense of human rights, preventing terrorism in the name of religion and promoting peace among

8. "New York Urban League," accessed September 19, 2016, *www.nyul.org*.

9. Congress of Racial Equality, accessed September 19, 2016, core-online.org/History/history.htm.

Christians Moslems and Jews. In the April 1998 edition of *Politics and Such*, I applauded The Givat Haviva Educational Foundation[10] for promoting cooperation between Arabs and Jews and sponsoring educational programs in the United States and abroad. The April 21, 1998, Givat Haviva Awards Dinner at the New York Plaza Hotel (hosted by the late ABC news anchor Peter Jennings) awarded Camelia Anwar Sadat and Kerry Kennedy for their continued efforts to promote world peace. *Politics and Such* applauded both of these women for their passionate, energetic and committed effort to protect human rights:

> *Kerry Kennedy founded the RFK Center for Human Rights in 1988 (which ensured protection of rights codified in the United Nations Declaration of Human Rights) and is co-chair of Amnesty International Leadership Council and on the Board of the Lawyers Committee for Human Rights. Camelia Sadat, though raised in the traditional Egyptian Muslim culture, was deeply moved by her father's commitment and ultimate sacrifice for world peace. She is a senior leader at Harvard's Institute of Politics and is the Vice President of the E Trealogo Organization that promotes peace through Judaism, Islam and Christianity. As a member of the Board of Givat Haviva, Camelia has helped in various negotiations between the Arabs and Israelis.* [11]

10. The Givat Haviva Educational Foundation, accessed September 19, 2016, www.givathaviva.org/.

11. Harriet Nesbitt, *Politics and Such, The Murray Hill News*, 1998.

The April 1996 edition of *Politics and Such* focused on the efforts of the International Rescue Committee's (IRC)[12] mission to provide emergency relief and to advocate for victims of violent conflict and oppression. During his lifetime, Angier Biddle Duke served as President of the IRC:

> *Thomas LaBreque[13], CEO of Chase Manhattan Bank, presented the (IRC) Distinguished Humanitarian Award to Tom Brokaw, anchor of NBC Nightly News.[14] Mrs. Andier Biddle Duke presented the Andier Biddle Duke Public Service Award to the Honorable John Whitehead, Chairman of the International Rescue Committee. George Plimpton emceed this event as only he can.[15]*

As a social columnist, I understand how important the constitutional right to freedom of the press is for the survival of a democratic society. The *Politics and Such*

12. International Rescue Committee, accessed September 19, 2016, www.rescue.org.

13. "Thomas G. Labrecque Smart Start Program," JPMorgan Chase & Co., accessed September 19, 2016, www.jpmorgan.com/pages/smartstart/ny. JPMorgan's Thomas G. Labrecque Smart Start Program annually offers ten New York City students a full-tuition scholarship, four years of rotational internships, a mentoring network and professional experience at any of eleven NYC universities. The program was originally created by Labrecque in 1992. The Thomas G. Labrecque Foundation was founded by the Labrecque family in 2003 in memory of their lost beloved. As part of the foundation, the Thomas G. Labrecque Classic *Run as One* event was launched by family members and friends to raise awareness and donations to fund research for finding a cure for lung cancer, raising up to $3.5 million to date.

14. Harriet Nesbitt, *Politics and Such*, *The Murray Hill News*, April 1996.

15. Harriet Nesbitt, *Politics and Such*, *The Murray Hill News*, April 1996.

columns (1996–1998) I quoted in this chapter reflect on politics, racial equality, the defense of human rights and the protection of the most vulnerable in society. I am publishing excerpts from *Politics and Such* in this edition because I believe, as an American citizen, that the public exchange of ideas is vital to the survival of the American Republic.

On November 24, 1998, at New York's Marriott Marquis Hotel, the 1998 Committee to Protect Journalists' International Press Freedom Awards[16] honored journalists around the world who have shown courage in defending press freedom. Media luminaries Ted Turner, Tom Brokaw, Dan Rather, Peter Jennings, and Jane Pauley presided. The April 1998 *Politics and Such* describes Bob Woodward praising Ben Bradley (belated editor of the Washington Post) and the Committee to Protect Journalists for promoting high journalistic standards:

> *A most stimulating evening of CPJ's International Press Freedom Awards was held at the Marriott Marquis . . . Ted Turner, Chairman of the Benefits committee, Tom Brokaw, Master of Ceremonies, and Dan Rather's opening remarks reiterated the urgency of realistic journalism which raises public awareness and truth to a higher level as opposed to irrelevant tabloid sensationalism.[17]*

The strong words of award recipient Grémah Boucar, of Niger's *Anfani* newspaper and magazine, and Radio Anfani, expressed courage and passion for freedom of the press. I am publishing this work to identify the need

16. "International Press Freedom Awards," Committee to Protect Journalists, accessed September 19, 2016, https://cpj.org/awards/1998/.

17. Harriet Nesbitt, *Politics and Such, The Murray Hill News,* April 1998.

for journalistic integrity. I applaud Anderson Cooper for maintaining high standards in broadcast journalism.

Politics and Such's commentary never breached social ethics or shaded the truth. As a columnist with a moral compass, I abhor the tabloid sensationalism that has marred the 2016 general election.

Scrooge Vann Rye Neck[18]

18. "Harriet's Scrooge Vann Rye Neck is the modern-day counterpart of Dickens' classic Christmas Carol villain: greedy, selfish, and lacking in mercy toward the destitute. [Priestley, Ignorance and Want."]Bob Cratchit carrying Tiny Tim are likenesses of Harriet's husband, Dick Nesbitt, and her son, Larry Nesbitt." DeFazio, *Keeping The Dream Alive*, 15.

Chapter Two

We will be judged as a society
by how we treat the most vulnerable.

I FOUNDED *Mothers for More Halfway Houses* because it is my deepest conviction that we will be judged as a society by how we treat our most vulnerable. Currently in Los Angeles and San Francisco there is an epidemic of homelessness. As the founder of *Mothers for More Halfway Houses*, it is my informed opinion that the majority of those homeless throughout the United States are mentally ill and among that population is a high ratio of HIV infected men and women. As a social column *Politics and Such* reported on the efforts of various organizations to help the physically and mentally ill.

The New York Academy of Medicine[1] held a December 1998 Celebration of Health at the Pierre Hotel. NYAM identifies urban health problems, defining and establishing solutions for them, and developing programs that build healthy urban communities. *Politics and Such*

1. The New York Academy of Medicine, accessed September 19, 2016, www.nyam.org/.

April 1998 edition covered NYAM's annual event hosted by television's distinguished anchor woman, Jane Pauley. *Politics and Such* commended the New York Academy of Medicine for awarding Dr. Martin Cherkasky a lifetime achievement award for his AIDS research:

> *Welcome also was the New York Academy of Medicine at the Pierre in their Celebration of Health hosted by Dateline anchor Jane Pauley[2] who awarded a citation in AIDS research as well as a lifetime achievement to Dr. Martin Cherkasky.* [3]

Miss Pauley's memoirs, *Skywriting: A Life Out of the Blue* published in 2004 explains her struggle with a chronic urban malaise- depression:

> *Approaching midlife, I became aware of a darkening feeling—was it something heavy on my heart or was something missing. Grateful as I am for the opportunities I have had, and especially for the people who came into my life as a result, I couldn't ignore that feeling. I had an impulse to begin a conversation with myself, through writing as if to see whether or not my fingers could get to the bottom of it.[4]*

Sky writing begins with an image or memory and seeing where the pen takes the writer. Without analyzing the process too much, writing out an image or a memory reveals and releases buried emotion.

2. Harriet Nesbitt, *Politics and Such*, *The Murray Hill News*, April 1998.

3. Harriet Nesbitt, *Politics and Such*, *The Murray Hill News*, April 1998.

4. Jane Pauley, *Skywriting: A Life Out of the Blue* (New York: Random House, 2004), xi.

I was glad to have gotten a photo of myself and Miss Pauley to include in the column. The successful treatment of depression is important to me and a focus of my work as director of *Mothers for More Halfway Houses.*

Children are a vulnerable population

In the April 1998 edition of *Politics and Such*, I commended CORE for honoring Michael Bolton whose foundation funded shelters across the nation for abused women and children:

> *The Congress of Racial Equality chaired by Roy Innes at the Sheraton filled its ballroom with luminaries Mayor and Mrs. Guiliani, James Earl Jones, and Connie Chung. Michael Bolton*[5] *received CORE's humanitarian award for distributing millions of dollars through his foundation to shelters across the nation that house battered women and their children.*[6]

According to the latest statistics, among all industrialized nations the United States has the largest number of homeless women and children. Not since the Depression have so many families been homeless. *Homeless families comprise 34% of the US homeless population. Among all homeless women, 60% have children under eighteen. 84% of families experiencing homelessness are female headed. Families of color are overrepresented in the homeless population. 43% are African American and 15% are Hispanic. 53% of homeless mothers do not have a high school*

5. The Michael Bolton Charities, accessed September 19, 2016, www.michaelboltoncharities.com/.

6. Harriet Nesbitt, *Politics and Such*, *The Murray Hill News*, April 1998.

diploma. *92% of homeless mothers have experienced physical or sexual abuse. Domestic violence is the principal cause of homelessness cited by single mother families.*[7] As a social columnist, and the founder of *Mothers For More Halfway Houses* these statistics concern me greatly.

Seniors are a vulnerable population.

I regularly attend a current events program at the Carter Burden Center for the Aging[8] in New York City. The leader of this forum provides fact sheets for seniors who attend so that they are able to stay informed on critical topics: Medicare and Medicaid regulations, services for seniors who are homebound and invalid, *Meals on Wheels*, as well as transportation and nursing services available for the elderly. Carter Burden provides counsel for the elderly, exercise classes, free films and a community for the large population of elderly residents in New York's Upper East Side.

According to the March 12, 2012, *US News and World Report* article entitled "Why Older Citizens Are More Likely to Vote:" *Seniors are more likely to vote than any other age group because retirees have more valuable government benefits to protect.*[9] In 2010 there were 1.4 million senior citizen voters in New York. I worked the

7. "Family Homelessness Facts," Green Doors, accessed September 19, 2016, http://www.greendoors.org/facts/family-homelessness.php.

8. Carter Burden Center, accessed September 19, 2016, www.carterburdencenter.org.

9. Emily Brandon, "Why Older Citizens Are More Likely to Vote," *US World and News Report*, March 19, 2012, accessed September 19, 2016, http://money.usnews.com/money/retirement/articles/2012/03/19/why-older-citizens-are-more-likely-to-vote.

polls in the general elections for several years in the East Side of Manhattan where I reside. My intention in writing this book is to provide a role model for seniors to participate in general elections. It is their right and civic responsibility. If seniors don't decide to vote on election day, that decision will be made for them.

I will conclude this chapter repeating my mantra: *We will be judged as a society by how we treat the most vulnerable.* I was fortunate to be brought up in the Great Depression by a father who was a distinguished judge and so my childhood was economically secure. My father "Honest Louis Lorence" instilled in me a strong awareness of the need for social justice. He insisted that greed was not the ultimate goal. My artistic tribute to Charles Dickens reflects the influence of his great social masterpiece *The Christmas Carol. Scrooge Vann* is depicted above a ragged destitute woman and the words of my late husband Dick Nesbitt are inscribed below: *Oh Material Microbe you will be blue, without your gold to follow you.*

Chapter Three

Social Media Is the Predictor
of the Postmodern Age.

IN MY LIFETIME I have experienced the dawn of television, mass telephone communication and digital reality on the world wide web. My life in New York City began before television was a household item and far before the invention of the internet, smart phone, ipod, ipad, cd or DVD. In my childhood, I connected with the outside world through the cinema, radio and newspaper journalism.

Cinema, newspaper journalism and radio were the predictors of my childhood. I grew up in an era when life each day began with a cup of morning coffee reading the daily news and listening to the radio. *Politics and Such* identified several organizations that were predictors of the millennial surge of social media.

Politics and Such (April 1998) covered

> *The Vision Awards Dinner of the New York Institute of Technology honoring Peter Max with a Doctoral Degree. The evening sparkled with good humor as Senator Ted Kennedy remarked that his Republican friends wished he painted*

> *full time. . . Larry King made the event so much*
> *more entertaining. As Mr. Redstone stated in his*
> *address, education and entertainment have a lot*
> *to do with each other .*[1]

In the millennial era the microscopic reach of cyberspace lends meaning to the popular phrase TMI (too much information)! Eighteen years ago, with great foresight, *Congresswoman Carolyn Maloney went to a hearing on the debt ceiling extension and voted for the Telecommunications Act.* [2]

The Telecommunications Act became effective immediately after President Clinton signed the bill into law on February 8, 1996.[3] Noting the historic nature of the bill, President Clinton stated that the legislation would *stimulate investment, promote competition, and provide open access for all citizens to the Information Superhighway.*[4] Its Title V, called the Communications Decency Act of 1996 (CDA) regulates the transmission of objectionable material over computer networks. The April 1998 *Politics and Such* edition,

> *. . .aligned Harriet Nesbitt's concerns with Via-*
> *com CEO Sumner Redstone for the future qual-*
> *ity of cyber security explaining the necessity of*
> *control over children's media exposure.*[5]

1. Harriet Nesbitt, *Politics and Such, The Murray Hill News*, April 1998.

2. Harriet Nesbitt, *Politics and Such, The Murray Hill News*, April 1998.

3. "Telecommunications Act of 1996," Federal Communications Commission, accessed September 19, 2016, www.fcc.gov/telecom. html.

4. Encyclopedia of Television, accessed September 19, 2016, http://www.museum.tv/eotvsection.php?entrycode=uspolicyt.

5. Harriet Nesbitt, *Politics and Such, "The Murray Hill News,*

The New York Institute of Technology is a private research university with a strong emphasis on technology and applied scientific research. At NYIT's February 1998 event, the best and brightest of Americans gathered to support NYIT for its environmental research of the relationship between electric vehicles and renewable energy charging stations. In these climatically intemperate times, it is relevant to note that the late Senator Ted Kennedy mentioned NYIT partnering with the United Nations to promote the International Water Conferences and Energy Conferences.

Politics and Such (April 1997) expressed concern for environmental protection:

> *So why do we continue to proliferate our environment with contaminants just to have conveniences and a luxurious way of life, when looking at the resulting floods, weather and climate changes.*[6]

April 1998.

6. Harriet Nesbitt, *Politics and Such*, *The Murray Hill News*, April 1997.

Sandy The Storm [7]

7. "Harriet's painting focused on a New York City couple who had nothing left but a porch.

Harriet completed *Sandy the Storm* to show concern for the devastating impact of climate change." DeFazio, *Keeping The Dream Alive*, 10.

In addition to his vast accomplishments in broadcast journalism, Ted Turner is an environmentalist who has restored wilderness lands and who, at the time of the 1998 UN Ambassadors Ball, had 4,000 buffalos roaming on his open prairie ranch. I described Ted as

> *A quintessential capitalist who has contributed to the betterment of humankind.*[8]

Politics and Such (April 1997) resonated with Turner's concern for balancing the environment:

> *Rather than strictly leaving the land untouched, we need to balance nature and go back to our roots to preserve the traditional web of life in swamp areas, as well as primeval forests.*[9]
>
> *Yelena Mikoloski, cable television host took a photo of me with Ted Turner who was honored at the United Nations Ambassador Ball*[10] *held in the Hall of Ocean Life at the Museum of Natural History. Behaviorally reticent but nevertheless a risk taker, Ted started CNN, purchased the Atlantic Braves, married Jane Fonda, conceived the Good Will Games, and launched the Cartoon Network and Turner Broadcasting.*[11]

In conclusion, social media is the predictor of the postmodern age. I chose to complete this work bringing the salient comments of *Politics and Such* to print as an ebook

8. Harriet Nesbitt, *Politics and Such, The Murray Hill News*, April 1997.

9. Harriet Nesbitt, *Politics and Such, The Murray Hill News*, April 1997.

10. "Ambassador's Ball," Hospitality Committee for United Nations Delegations, Inc., accessed September 19, 2016, http://www.hcund.org/ball.html.

11. Harriet Nesbitt, *Politics and Such, The Murray Hill News*, February 1998.

hoping that my reflections will inspire others to express themselves via electronic and digital media and make a difference.

CHAPTER FOUR

Politics and Such 1996 list
of most fascinating women.

MY ANNUAL LIST OF most fascinating women of 1996 began with Madeline Albright, the newly appointed Secretary of State. *Madeleine Albright Madeleine Korbelová Albright was the first woman to become the United States Secretary of State. She was appointed by US President Bill Clinton on December 5, 1996, and was unanimously confirmed by a U.S. Senate vote of 99–0. She was sworn in on January 23, 1997.*[1]

Politics and Such (April 1996) identified *Albright's firmness of purpose as Chief United Nations Delegate that served as an advantage in this most important job in the Clinton administration.*[2] Madam Secretary Albright demonstrated great authority as the first female secretary of state. Her model of diplomacy and strength and good humor were impressive.

1. Harriet Nesbitt, *Politics and Such*, *The Murray Hill News*, February 1998.

2. Harriet Nesbitt, *Politics and Such*, *The Murray Hill News*, April 1996.

On Sunday March 3, 1996, a photographic tribute to slain Prime Minister Yitzak Rabin was held at a private gallery near the United Nations in New York. Leah Rabin attended. Her story is one of extreme bravery and courage. *Leah Rabin (4/8/1928 –11/12/2000) was the widow of Israeli Prime Minister Yitzhak Rabin, who was assassinated in 1995 by a terrorist in Jerusalem.*[3]

She spoke briefly at this event expressing the heartfelt belief that good would overcome the evil of terrorist acts. She was a passionate, energetic, extremely down to earth and a very approachable woman. You could not meet Leah Rabin without wanting to be a better person.

In the April 1996 edition of *Politics and Such*, I recognized the impact of meeting Leah Rabin on my life: *For valor and dignity, Leah Rabin, widow of Israel's slain prime minister, receives high tribute.* [4]

Kathy Lee Gifford is one of the most durable and successful television personalities of our time. She is a television host, singer, songwriter and actress, best known for her 15-year run (1985–2000) on the talk show *Live with Regis and Kathie Lee*, which she co-hosted with Regis Philbin.

> *She has received 11 Daytime Emmy nominations and won her first Daytime Emmy in 2010 as part of The Today Show team. On April 7, 2008, Gifford began co-hosting the fourth hour of NBC's Today Show, alongside Hoda Kotb.*[5]

3. Wikipedia, Leah Rabin, https://en.wikipedia.org/wiki/Leah_Rabin; accessed August 31, 2025.

4. Wikipedia, Madeleine Albright, https://en.wikipedia.org/wiki/Madeleine Albright. accessed, August 31, 2025.

5. *Wikipedia,* Kathie Lee Gifford, accessed September 19, 2016, https://en.wikipedia.org/wiki/Kathie_Lee_Gifford.

In 1996, she made *Politics and Such* list of most fascinating women for founding Cassidy Place. Kathie Lee Gifford is passionate and committed to help children through the foundation of Cassidy Place, Cody House and the Association to Benefit Children. Named for her daughter Cassidy, Cassidy Place is the home of the Association to Benefit Children's national children's advocacy. Its programs provide family support services, a day care center for homeless children, a mentoring program which pairs homeless children with adults from all walks of life and a large therapeutic day nursery. Cassidy Place serves poor children with disabling conditions including HIV and AIDS.

> *Kathy Lee Gifford gets my vote for her commitment to Cassidy Place.*[6]

Mary Tyler Moore is an American actress, primarily known for her roles in television sitcoms. *She is best known for The Mary Tyler Moore Show (1970–77),* in which she starred as Mary Richards, a 30-something single woman who worked as a local news producer in Minneapolis, and for her earlier role as *Laura Petrie (Dick Van Dyke's wife) on The Dick Van Dyke Show (1961–66).*[7]

Mary Tyler Moore made the *Politics and Such 1996* list of most fascinating women because she has been active in charity work and various political causes, particularly around the issues of animal rights and Diabetes Mellitus Type 1. She is the International Chairman of the Juvenile

6. Harriet Nesbitt, *Politics and Such, The Murray Hill News*, April 1996.

7. "She is best known for The Mary Tyler Moore Show (1970–77)," "Laura Petrie (Dick Van Dyke's wife) on *The Dick Van Dyke Show* (1961–66)." Wikipedia, "Mary Tyler Moore," accessed September 19, 2016, https://en.m.wikipedia.org/wiki/Mary _Tyler Moore.

Diabetes Research Foundation:[8] *Mary Tyler Moore gets my personal thanks for her philanthropic and personal victory over diabetes.*[9]

I wrote this chapter to encourage all women to fulfill their destiny. I bore two wonderful sons out of my womb but through the years many young women have been like daughters to me. I am mentioning Edith Ariel, Demetria Daniels, Jeanne DeFazio, Georgian Macri and April Shenandoah to name a few. I supported these women in their early years in their goals as artists and authors. I encouraged each one of them to make a difference. I am happy to say they all have distinguished themselves as artists and authors. As a woman and an artist, I understand how important encouragement and support can be. As a young artist, I was fortunate to study and work as an artist in Paris, Mexico and New York. I was educated at the Ecole des Beaux Arts in Paris and the Instituto San Miguel d'Allende in Mexico. At New York City's Art League, I received seven scholarships to become an assistant instructor and Life Member. I received a National Academy Scholarship becoming an Assistant Instructor. I have served as an Assistant Instructor (Monitor) at the American Art School.

My art has been exhibited at the Eighth Street Gallery, Empire State Building; Fleet Bank; Gallery 62, the Keane Mason Gallery; the Key Gallery on 57th Street; the Showcase Artist Monthly and Lincoln Center in New York City, New York; the New Jersey State Museum of the Arts, Cord Gallery Southampton LI, NY.; the Palm Beach

8. Juvenile Diabetes Research Foundation, accessed September 19, 2016, *www.jdf.org/*.

9. Harriet Nesbitt, *Politics and Such*, *The Murray Hill News*, April 1996.

Towers; the Parrish Art Museum, Marco Polo Gallery, Greenwich, CT; and the Womanart Gallery.

I have been awarded the Fire Island Art Association 1st Senior Prize and 2nd Senior Prize (twice).

My art is in the following collections:

M.P. Grace II of the WR Grace family, Huntington Hartford, Lady Victoria Sassoon, Mrs. Amory Haskell, Jr., Mayor Earl E.T. Smith, Palm Beach, Robert Mitchum, Erin O'Brian, Pres. Greenwich, CT. Polo Assn., Martin Gainsbrugh, Chief Economist, Solar Surgical Instrument Co., National Industrial Conference Board, E.P. DeBeteta, Minister of Finance Mexico, Julie Wilson, Mr. and Mrs. Joseph Hermes, Simon Milner, Sorbonne and Paris Art Critic, Premier Earl Gairy, Greneda, WI, La Guardia and Wagner Mayoral Archives,[10] Grace Institute, NYC, NY, Cornell University, Comptroller, and the Beverly Historical Society Revolutionary War Exhibit.[11]

10. Harriet Nesbitt's portrait of Mayor Koch is included in The La Guardia Wagner Collection. La Guardia and Wagner Archives. https://www.laguardiawagnerarchive.lagcc.cuny.edu/pages/Image-DetailNew.aspx.

11. Harriet Nesbitt's portrait of General Putnam is included in The Beverly Historical Society's Revolutionary War Collection. https://historicbeverly.net/.

The Atomic Madonna [12]

12. "Bellini's Madonna and Child inspired her [Harriet Nesbitt] to create *The Atomic Madonna*. It is a self-portrait of Harriet and her son Larry. The contrast of the Prince of Peace and his mother with the nuclear mushroom cloud in the background depicts her concern for the danger of nuclear war and annihilation." DeFazio, *Keeping The Dream Alive,* 21.

CONCLUSION

Dr. Pangloss, Candide's eternal optimist,
believed that in spite of everything it is the
best of all possible worlds. Candide (Voltaire)[1]

EACH INDIVIDUAL REPRESENTED IN *Politics and Such* passionately and energetically advanced the cause of humankind. It has been my honor to meet them and to reflect on their service to humankind. Their impact on my life has been transformational.

Dr. Pangloss, the eternal optimist, in Voltaire's satire *Candide* believed that in spite of everything it is the best of all possible worlds. I believe that every challenge provides an open door. My son Larry died tragically and at his death I founded Mother's For More Halfway Houses so that those struggling with mental illness have shelter to heal. Meeting Mother Teresa inspired me to continue work as founder of MMHH. In conclusion I want to remind readers of her words:

1. Wikipedia, "Candide," accessed September 19, 2016, https://en.m.wikipedia.org/wiki/Candide.

> . . .at the hour of death we are going to be judged
> on what we have been to the poor, to the hungry,
> naked, the homeless, and he (Jesus) makes him-
> self that hungry one, that naked one, that home-
> less one, not only hungry for bread, but hungry
> for love, not only naked for a piece of cloth, but
> naked of that human dignity, not only homeless
> for a room to live, but homeless for that being
> forgotten, been unloved, uncared, being nobody
> to nobody, having forgotten what is human love,
> what is human touch, what is to be loved by
> somebody, and he says: Whatever you did to the
> least of these my brethren, you did it to me.[2]

Mother Teresa ended her speech quoting Jesus: *Whatever you did to the least of these my brethren, you did it to me.*[3] My son Larry, like Mother Teresa, understood the importance of spiritual guidance. He left me his Bible and in times of discouragement and when I still miss him more than I can bear I open it as a point of contact. I feel Larry's presence every day and especially when I am in contact with my son Roger. Larry did not die in vain. His memory lives on through the work of *Mothers for More Halfway Houses.*

2. "Mother Teresa—Acceptance Speech," Nobelprize.org, accessed September 19, 2016, http://www.nobelprize.org/nobel_prizes/peace/laureates/1979/teresa-acceptance.html.

3. Matthew 25:40 KJV.

About the Authors

Julia C. Davis holds an EDM from the Harvard Graduate School of Education and an EDM from Bouve College of Health Sciences at Northeastern University. She has held teaching certificates in New York, Massachusetts, and the District of Columbia and has been certified as an Assistant Principal and as an Assistant Special Education Supervisor. Julia has taught in the public and private sector in community-based programs including METCO, Summer STEP opportunities for underrepresented populations in science and technology and Head Start. She has served as a member of Parent's Advocacy Group for Massachusetts supporting FAPE and mainstreaming Special Education students. She has taught pre-K through all 12 grades, Adult Non- Readers, Limited English Language Learners and GED Preparation courses. Julia taught internationally as an undergraduate exchange student in a Special Education Program based in Newnham on Severn, Gloucester shire, England, which operated under the auspices of Antioch College in Ohio. Julia and her husband Dan have three children and three grandchildren. They attend the International Family Church in North Reading, Massachusetts.

Jeanne DeFazio is a former SAG/AFTRA (Screen Actors Guild—American Federation of Television and Radio Artists) actress of Spanish Italian descent, who played supporting parts in theater, movies, and television series, then served the marginalized in the drama of real life. She became a teacher of second language-learner children in the barrios of San Diego. She completed a BA in History at the University of California, Davis, MAR in Theology at Gordon- Conwell Theological Seminary, and a Cal State Teach English Language Learners program. From 2009 to 2024, she served as an Athanasian Teaching Scholar at Gordon-Conwell's multicultural Boston Center for Urban Ministerial Education.

Olga Soler is director/writer and performer for Estuary Ministries, a Christ-centered performing arts ministry dealing with biblical themes, inner healing, abuse, and addictive problems. The art forms used include drama, dance, storytelling, mime, comedy, graphic arts, writing, film, and song. Olga attended the High School of Performing Arts ("Fame"), the Lee Strasberg Theater Institute, and the Herbert Berghof Studios, in New York City. She has performed widely at conferences, churches, prisons, coffee houses, support groups, youth groups, and retreats and has even performed on the streets, at secular colleges, and in worship services across the United States and the United Kingdom. She holds degrees in education and communications with equivalent studies in theology and psychology. She studied for two years at Gordon Conwell Theological Seminary. She has designed and conducted the workshops "Dance Alive" and "Trauma Drama" at many Christian recovery conferences. She wrote the curriculum for and conducted discovery groups for addicts at the Boston Rescue Mission, using the arts to help them process aspects of their recovery. She also conducts workshops for Christian drama and dance in many churches of all denominations. Using Paulo Freire's "pedagogy of the oppressed," she wrote a script for the "Mosaics" group of parents helping their children who have been victims of sexual abuse through the court system and assisted them in filming the script for a documentary. She performed and coauthored scripts for four years with the "Team" Christian ministry in Massachusetts and conducted eight full-scale multimedia presentations out of the Rio Ondo Arts Place in Woburn, Massachusetts, including "Voice of the Martyrs," "Techno Easter," and "Clean Comedy Night." She has directed and choreographed entire productions at universities and colleges, including *A Man for All Seasons, Jane Eyre, Amal and the Night Visitors*, and (by permission of the author) Calvin Miller's *The Singer*. She wrote and illustrated the book *Epistle to the Magadalenes* and has conducted retreats for women using the book accompanied by dramatic presentation. She is the author of many other books and assorted screenplays. She is the proud mother of three wonderful children, Cielo, Reva, and Ransom. She lives in Massachusetts with her husband, Chris, and her Japanese Chin (dog), Kiji. Email Olga at fleursavag@yahoo.com,

Bibliography

Brainy Quote. "Donald Trump." Accessed September 19, 2016. http: //www.brainyquote.com/quotes/authors/d/donald_trump_2. html#z3TtPvlsu5Umi2QS.99.

Brandon, Emily. "Why Older Citizens Are More Likely to Vote." *US World and News Report*. March 19, 2012. Accessed September 19, 2016. http://money.usnews.com/money/retirement/articles /2012/03/19/why-older-citizens-are-more-likely-to-vote.

Carter Burden Center. Accessed September 19, 2016, www. carterburdencenter.org.

Committee to Protect Journalists. "International Press Freedom Awards." Accessed September 19, 2016, https://cpj.org/awards /1998/.

Congress of Racial Equality. "History." Accessed September 19, 2016, www.core-online.org/History/history.htm.

DeFazio, Jeanne. *Keeping The Dream Alive: A Reflection on The Art Of Harriet Lorence Nesbitt*. Eugene, OR: Resource Publications, 2019.

Forrester, Meg. "What We Know About the Minnesota School Shooting Suspect Robin Westman." ABC News, August 28, 2025. https://abcnews.go.com/US/minnesota-school-shooting -suspect-robin-westman/story?id=125029777.

The Givat Haviva Educational Foundation. Accessed September 19, 2016, www.givathaviva.org/.

Green Doors. "Family Homelessness Facts." Accessed September 19, 2016, http://www.greendoors.org/facts/family-homelessness.php.

Hospitality Committee for United Nations Delegations, Inc. "Ambassador's Ball." Accessed September 19, 2016, http://www .hcund.org/ball.html.

JPMorgan Chase & Co. "Thomas G. Labrecque Smart Start Program." Accessed September 19, 2016. www.jpmorgan.com/pages/smartstart/ny.

Juvenile Diabetes Research Foundation. Accessed September 19, 2016, www.jdf.org/.

Madigan, Tim. "Van Cliburn: The Texan Who Conquered Russia." Fort Worth StarTelegram, February 27, 2013. https://www.star-telegram.com/living/family/moms/article3834080.html.

Mothers For More Halfway Houses Inc. Accessed September 19, 2016. http://www.charityblossom.org/nonprofit/mothers-for-more-halfway-houses-inc-new-york-ny-10065-harriet-nesbitt-133229931/.

Nesbitt, Harriet. "Politics and Such." *The Murray Hill News*. April 1996, 1997, 1998, February 1998.

Nobelprize.org. "Mother Teresa—Acceptance Speech." Accessed September 19, 2016. http://www.nobelprize.org/nobel_prizes/peace/laureates/1979/teresa-acceptance.html.

The Beverly Historical Society. "The American Revolution: A Story of the War in 28 Paintings." https://historicbeverly.net/event/the-american-revolution-a-story-of-the-war-in-28-paintings/.

The La Guardia Wagner Archives. https://www.laguardiawagnerarchive.lagcc.cuny.edu/pages/ImageDetailNew.aspx.

The New York Academy of Medicine. Accessed September 19, 2016, www.nyam.org/.

New York Institute of Technology. Accessed September 19, 2016, nyit.edu.

New York Urban League. Accessed September 19, 2016, www.nyul.org.

Pauley, Jane. *Skywriting: A Life Out of the Blue*. New York: Random House, 2001.

Priestley, Chris. "Ignorance and Want: Why Charles Dickens's A Christmas Carol Is as Relevant Today as Ever." *The Guardian*, December 23, 2015. https://www.theguardian.com/childrens-books-site/2015/dec/23/ignorance-and-want-why-charles-dickenss-a-christmas-carol-is-as-relevant-today-as-ever.

Wikipedia, The Free Encyclopedia. "Candide." Accessed September 19, 2016. https://en.m.wikepedia.org/wiki/Candide.

———. "Kathie Lee Gifford." Accessed September 19, 2016. https://en.wikipedia.org/wiki/Kathie_Lee_Gifford.

———. "Leah Rabin." Accessed August 31, 2025. https://en.wikipedia.org/wiki/Leah_Rabin.

―――. "Madeleine Albright." Accessed August 31, 2025. https://en.wikipedia.org/wiki/Madeleine Albright.

―――. "Mary Tyler Moore." Accessed September 19, 2016. https://en.m.wikepedia.org/wiki/Mary _Tyler Moore.

―――. "Missionaries of Charity." https://en.wikipedia.org/wiki/Missionaries_of_Charity.

―――. "Mother Teresa." Accessed September 19, 2016. https://en.m.wikepedia.org/wiki/Mother Teresa.